I Cannot Live Without You

BY KEITH HILL

CLASSICS OF WORLD MYSTICISM

The Bhagavad Gita: A new poetic translation

Interpretations of Desire:
Mystical love poems by the Sufi master Ibn 'Arabi

Psalms of Exile and Return:
A journey in search of inner healing and unity

I Cannot Live Without You:
Selected Poetry of Mirabai and Kabir

POETRY

The Ecstasy of Cabeza de Vaca

The Lounging Lizard Poet of the Floating World

FICTION

Puck of the Starways

Blue Kisses

NON-FICTION

The New Mysticism

The God Revolution

Striving To Be Human

What's Really Going On?

Where Do I Go When I Meditate?

How Did I End Up Here?

Experimental Spirituality

Practical Spirituality

Psychological Spirituality

I Cannot Live Without You

Selected Poetry of Mirabai and Kabir

ILLUSTRATIONS BY
Sigrid Saga

Translations BY
Keith Hill

attar ‖ books

First published in 2021 by Attar Books
Auckland, New Zealand

Paperback ISBN 978-0-9951333-3-4
Ebook ISBN 978-0-9951333-4-1

Cover image: Shutterstock

Attar Books is a New Zealand publisher which focuses on work
that explores today's spiritual experiences, culture, concepts and
practices. For more information visit our website:

www.attarbooks.com

Dedicated to the memory of
Shri Mauniji Maharaj
a yogi of rare insight and wisdom

Contents

2 Upanishads

7 Poems by Kabir

Appendices

Introduction

Mirabai and Kabir are not only two of India's greatest poets, they are among the finest mystical poets in all world literature. The exquisite devotional lyrics of Mirabai, still sung in India today, and the knotty, acerbic sayings of Kabir, which continue to resonate with seekers of all spiritual traditions, are on a par with the work of the other great spiritual artists of the same era—the ecstatic poems of St John of the Cross, the visionary art and music of Abbess Hildegard of Bingen, the revolutionary frescos of Giotto, the mystic writings of St Teresa of Avilra, and the lyricism of the great Sufi poets Rumi, Hafiz and Ibn 'Arabi.

However, a gulf separates contemporary Western culture from that of pre-modern India. The following biographical notes aim to conjure in the reader a sense of the very different world in which Mirabai and Kabir lived. They are followed by an introduction to the spiritual philosophy and practices that lie behind the poets' work, including the doctrines of Vedanta as embodied in the Upanishads. These notes are followed by a description of how this collection came to be.

The life of Mirabai

Legend says that, as a baby, Mira was found in a river near Kurki, in Rajasthan, and was taken into the household of the local king, Ratansi. The truth is somewhat more prosaic. Mira was born on 15 April 1498, in Bajoli, a small village six miles south-east of Degana Junction, on what is now the Delhi-Jodhpur railway line. Both her parents were of royal lineage, her father being Ratansi Dudawat, her mother, Kusumb Kanwar. On Mira's birth, Ratansi had a new palace built at Kurki which became her home for her early years. An interesting story relates a supposed incident from this time. It is said that one day Mira saw a marriage party and, on asking what was happening, the event was explained to her. Mira then asked who her husband was. Perhaps jokingly, perhaps seriously, her mother said Krishna. From that day, Mira began worshipping Krishna as her husband.

While Mira was still a child, her mother died. Viramdeo, Mira's father's oldest brother, then called her to live with him. Merta became her home. A story from these years indicates the strength of her devotion. Every day Mira accompanied the king to the temple where they offered milk to the statue of Krishna. One day the king was unable to attend, so Mira took the milk alone. She asked Krishna to accept the milk, but nothing happened. Then she pleaded, saying he should drink or the king would become angry with her. Krishna then appeared from within the statue and drank the milk. Later, Mira told the king what had happened but he didn't believe her; so again she took the milk, and again Krishna appeared and drank it. While we don't know why Mira chose Krishna to worship rather than another form of God, we do know a saint gave Mira a statue of Krishna, which she worshipped daily. This statue, called Saligram, now rests near the statue of Charbhuja, in the Mira temple at Merta.

The next significant event in Mira's life occurred in 1517 when, at the age of nineteen, she was married to Bhoj Raj

Sangawat, son of the Maharana of Mewar. The marriage bore no children and ended six years later, on her husband's death in 1523. Mira remained in the household of her parents-in-law, who lived in Chittore, under the rule of her brother-in-law, Ranaji. Whether the references in her poems to Ranaji trying to poison her are literal or metaphorical, her life there was difficult. After a final conflict in 1534, she left, never to return. This event in Mira's life is recorded in the fourth of the following poems.

Once again, Merta became Mira's home, but intermittently, for during those years she traveled a great deal, regularly visiting the holy cities of Pushkar, Vrindaban and Dwarika. A final story relates to those years.

Mira had gone travelling to Dwarika, so the anxious king of Merta sent his men to bring her back. Meeting them, Mira agreed to return, but only after she had worshipped Krishna. Thus, she entered the temple and the men waited outside. Some time passed. At last, frustrated by the delay they went inside, but to their surprise Mira had disappeared. All they found was her cloth hanging from the statue of Krishna. In the depths of her devotion she had become one with her lord. During one of her visits to Dwarika Mira died. The year was 1547. She was 49 years old.

The life of Kabir

We know less about Kabir's life than we do about Mirabai's, and even that comes to us not via historical record, but through the haze of oral legend. Some of Kabir's followers claim he lived from 1205 to 1505 CE. Scholars variously date his birth from 1437 to 1497, and his death between 1505 and 1575.

As with Mira, legend says of Kabir's birth that he was

found as a baby in a river in or near Benares, in this case by a Muslim couple who then adopted him as their own. An alternative birth story is that Kabir was born to a widowed Brahman, and that his (miraculous) birth had been foretold by Ramananda, Kabir's eventual guru. Whether he was adopted no one knows, but when his reputation became established both Hindus and Muslims claimed him as a saint.

Details of Kabir's spiritual development are equally scarce. One tradition maintains that he taught from an early age but because he lacked a guru people laughed at him, refusing to accept he had any authority to teach. Consequently, he decided he needed a guru. He was drawn to Ramananda (c. 1400–1480), who was leading a revival of Vedic knowledge in Benares. But there was one obstacle to Kabir becoming Ramananda's pupil: Kabir was a Muslim, and Indian Muslims were not accepted by Indian Hindu teachers.

Accordingly, so the story goes, Kabir hid on the steps down which Ramananda walked on the way to his daily bath. Stumbling over Kabir, in surprise he uttered, "Ram!" This allowed Kabir to claim he had been initiated and was now Ramananda's pupil. Later in his life Kabir's guru was possibly the equally revered Sufi Pir, Takki of Jhansi.

Kabir was no desert ascetic. He was married, most likely at a young age as was the custom, and had a son and a daughter. One story relates that when Loi, Kabir's wife, first met him she asked him what his caste was, and he replied, "Kabir." She then asked what his religion was. Again he responded, "Kabir." Finally, she asked what cloth he wore. Yet again came the answer, "Kabir." Kabir's outlook was his own, derived from his spiritual experiences. In expressing his vision, he bluntly criticized both Muslims and Hindus for their blind attachment to dogma and ritual forms. Naturally this led to conflict, not only with the Brahman authorities in Benares, but with the ordinary believers he met during his journeys from village to village. A story relates that to counteract the popular animosity he hired a prostitute to approach him in these various villages to try to seduce him. When the people saw he was not seduced, but rather she was converted to his teaching, they began calling him a saint. Thereafter, the animosity declined in intensity.

Another story shows Kabir's ability to exploit a situation for teaching purposes. One day a fakir visited Kabir to pay his respects, but on finding a pig tied to a peg in the yard he became upset. He said that since pigs are unholy, he couldn't stay. Kabir responded: "There are five pigs inside the body. Why don't you hate these pigs too, and refuse to sit with them?" Immediately, the fakir bowed his head and begged to become Kabir's pupil.

Despite his acumen, the Brahman authorities finally did catch up with Kabir. Following a report that he had used magic to raise a person from the dead, the Brahmans complained to the ruler of Benares, Sikander Lodi, demanding retribution. Kabir was a Muslim, and so was not under their religious jurisdiction. Nonetheless, Sikander Lodi recognized the difficulties such a free-thinker posed and Kabir was banished. He continued travelling between various northern Indian cities and villages, and probably died in Maghar, near Gorakhpur.

After Kabir's death, both Hindus and Muslims claimed the body. Legend says, however, that when they lifted the death-shroud all they found were two flowers. Each group took one flower, and both were satisfied. Hindus and Muslims have continued to revere Kabir ever since.

The significance of Vedanta

India's most ancient religious texts are the Vedas. Their source materials cannot be dated, but they likely circulated in oral form for centuries before being written down around 500 BCE. The Vedas contain five varieties of material: mythological narratives recounting the activites of the gods, prayers to the gods, descriptions of religious rituals, celebratory hymns, and wisdom texts called Upanishads. The Upanishads are also known as Vedanta, which literally means "the end of the Vedas", on the grounds they complete the Vedas, offering profound metaphysical views of reality and humanity's spiritual nature. Inspired by these early Upanishads, over the following millenia over two hundred more were written. The *Muktika Upanishad* identifies one hundred and eight Upanishads as canonical. However, the thirteen oldest Upanishads, which are included in the Vedas, are agreed to be the major Upanishads.

Sometime between 500 and 200 BCE, the author (or authors) of the *Brahma Sutras* collated and systematised the metaphysical ideas explored in the Upanishads—again dates are uncertain, with the text possibly reaching its current form as late as the fifth century CE. During the same period, the author (or authors) of the *Bhagavad Gita* created a syncretic text that wove the Upanishads' metaphysics, Samkhya philosophy, Vedic mythology, and yogic practices, into a sequence of eighteen discourses. These three texts—the Upanishads, *Brahma Sutras* and *Bhagavad Gita*—provide the foundational books for Vedanta, and have been adopted as such by all Indian philosophic and mystic schools—given Vedanta's ideas developed in parallel to, and frequently overlap with, the earliest Jain and Buddhist Pali texts.

The two Upanishads presented here, the *Isha Upanishad*

and *Kena Upanishad*, are among the thirteen major Upanishads. They are also two of the shortest, and are among just five written wholly in verse. The principal theme that unites all the canonical Upanishads is two-fold: reality is the manifestation of, and exists within, Brahman, the Absolute source of all; and atman, the spiritual self within, is identical with Brahman. This identical nature means that knowledge of atman leads to knowledge of Brahman—with the caveat that Brahman, being the vast, indefinable Absolute, is ultimately unknowable. Thus the spiritual seeker's goal, as presented in the Upanishds, is direct spiritual knowledge of the Self, which in turn makes possible personal enounters with Brahman.

Isha Upanishad begins by asserting that the Self that underpins everything existing is Brahman. If we ignore this reality by placing other aspects of human experience at the centre of our lives—such as possessions, status, money, work, family—we will be reborn into difficult situations. While the world's religions typically view humanity as being condemned due to the sinfulness that results when we engage in evil thoughts and actions, in the Upanishads sin is viewed as resulting from our ignorance of the Self. It is by renouncing our *attachment* to the manifold aspects of everyday life, rather than renouncing those aspects themselves, that we achieve knowledge of Brahman as our Self. This knowledge is achieved and sustained when we see Brahman in everything around us.

Kena Upanishad takes up this same theme, but extends it in a different direction. Where *Isha Upanishad* explores our relationship to what is around us, and so is outwardly directed, *Kena Upanishad* examines the nature of our inner experience of the external world. It directs us to consider the mysterious force that exists within us, that which hears what we hear, sees what we see, tastes what we taste, and so forth. This is the Self that exists behind and beyond our everyday self. True knowledge involves knowing that Self, to which we therefore should pay homage, rather than to the gods human beings conceive of as acting in, rather than behind, the physical world.

To reinforce this view, the author offers a tale in which Brahman challenges three of India's principal gods—Agni (the god of fire), Vayu (the god of wind and breath), and Indra (the king of heaven)—asking them to approach a mysterious spirit and discover the spirit's naure. Each god is sufficiently powerful to approach it, but none learns who it is. However, Indra is considered learn the most, because when he approaches he perceives the spirit is Uma, who, among her numerous manifestations and names, embodies knowledge of Brahman. *Kena Upanishad* concludes by asserting that what exists behind our breath, which we experience through meditation, is the ultimate goal of all knowledge. Hence it is spiritual knowledge, not religious beliefs or rituals, which enlighten and save us. In a reiteration of the teaching of *Isha Upanishad*, knowledge is considered to save because it is grounded in direct experience of atman, our spiritual self that itself is a manifestation of the ultimate Self.

Appreciation of the teachings of Vedanta ebbed and flowed over the centuries that followed their composition, due to their being taught by rote, being over-intellectualised, or simply being ignored. However, in the eighth century CE a significant revival of Vedanta occurred when Shankara took on the task of expounding the doctrine of Advaita Vedanta, the mystical monist view that nothing exists but Brahman. This view is also known as non-dualism. Shankara likely lived only into his thirties (his birth and death cannot be verified), but through his tireless travelling and debating, through the ashrams he established, and through the commentaries he wrote on the major Upanishads, on the *Brahma Sutras*, and on the *Bhagavad Gita*, he had a profound impact on subsequent Indian philosophy and spirituality.

Another influential exponent of Vedanta was Chaitanya (c. 1486–1534 CE). A contemporary of Mirabai, Chaitanya was originally initiated into Shankara's monastic tradition. However, he later became a Vaishnava, worshipping Vishnu as a manifestation of Brahman. One of Vishnu's avatars is Krishna, who Chaitanya ecstatically worshipped in song and dance. Indeed, he so intensely identified with Krishna that his followers came to view Chaitanya himself as a physical embodiment of his divine lord.

Philosophically, Chaitanya taught a form of Vedanta called Achintya–Bheda–Abheda. Many different Vedantic schools developed over the centuries as seekers sought to re-councile the absolute intellectual monism of Advaita Vedanta with the complexities of living in the physical world with its unavoidable divisions and oppositions. The non-dualist Shankara taught that Brahman and atman, Creator and created, the Absolute and conditioned reality, were one and the same. In contrast, other Indian thinkers argued an unbridgeable separation exists between Brahman and atman, Creator and created, so they adopted a extreme dualism. Chaitanya reconciled both positions, teaching that Krishna is simultaneously separate from, and united with, His ecstatic worshippers. This view had an impact on one of Kabir's teachers, Ramananda.

During the fourteenth century Ramananda led a spiritual revival in the city of Varanasi, in Uttar Pradesh. With this revival came a number of religious and social reforms. While Ramananda personally practised traditional Vedic asceticism, he rejected traditional religous and caste distinctions, teaching that all believers worshipped the same God. Ramananda's outlook was shaped during his youth when he was exposed to the teaching of Ramanuja (c. 1017–1137 CE), a reformer who rejected the predominant stilted, heavily ritualised and intellectualised Vedic religion of his day. Ramanuja taught a philosophy of qualified non-dualism. Non-dualist worshippers are required to look past differences in form to perceive the one Absolute, which lies behind all manifestations. However, in practice few devotees can kneel to an abstraction; most require a concrete form on which to focus their worship. Vishnu is the god most cited in the Vedas, so Ramanuja taught that Vishnu, particularly Vishnu in the form of Narayana, should be the object of worship. *Nara* means water, while *ayana* means flowing, or movement. Thus *Narayana* indicates that the cosmos is like an undulating ocean: we ordinarily perceive the waves and not the ocean currents that drive the waves, yet they are present and are one with the waves. This view underpins Ramanuja's advocacy of qualified non-dualism: that while all existence is ultimately one, just as we recognise a wave yet know it is part of the ocean, so we may validly view the Absolute as manifesting in particular forms and characters. Hence we can validly worship a particular visible form, knowing the "behind" it is the invisible Absolute.

Ramananda's outlook included all this. However, by the time he began teaching Sufi thought, and particularly the love ethic that lies at the heart of the poetry and philosophy of the Persian Sufis, was having an impact on Indian bhakti worship. Coupling this development to the religious reforms begun by Ramanuja, Ramananda brought together three significant innovations: using music, dance, and song in religious devotion; promoting the writing of spiritual poetry in local dialects, rather than the formal Sanskrit used by Brahman priests; and propagating popular oral literature that the illiterate could enjoy and learn from. This last was in contrast to religious and philosophic texts that only the more educated, higher castes could read.

This merging of Sufi devotional literature with traditional bhakti worship not only meant that the love ethic gave added intensity to India's religious practices, it provided a common ground for Hindus and Muslims to meet. Thus in Ramananda's school yogis and Sufis, ascetics and householders, scholars and the uneducated, met openly to discuss the intricacies of God-realisation.

The influence on Mirabai and Kabir

Mirabai and Kabir created poetry in an environment impacted by these social, philosophic and literary shifts. Mirabai begins many of her poems by representing an emotional situation drawn from her life, which she then spiritually transcends. In contrast, Kabir often starts his poems with an abstract concept, then presents a series of examples to show how that concept manifests in everyday experience. Nonetheless, they share a number of key ideas and practices.

First is bhakti. Bhakti is a devotional practice by which a seeker strives to devote herself or himself to a particular form of Deity. As the practice intensifies, the worshipper transcends the particular form, seeing all forms, indeed the world itself, as a manifestation of Deity. Eventually, the worshipper's consciousness becomes so infused that there is no longer a perception of manifested Deity and worshipper: all is One. This process of growing from particular to universal, from physical statue to transcendent reality, Mirabai evocatively presents in her poems. Psychologically, bhakti also offers the seeker a way of transcending the limits of personality. This is achieved because the worshipper's intensity of devotion and love burns away the dross of limiting emotions and attitudes, such as selfishness, fear, envy, desire, resentment, self-pity, and so on. Eventually, after a requisite quality of inner purification is achieved, the seeker transcends her or his limited, sense-focused self and sees God in and as all.

Where Mirabai's poems provide very sensual images of Krishna as her beloved, Kabir refers to God in the form of Ram, which is one of India's most common divine names. However for Kabir, and unlike Mirabai, in the poems offered here Ram has no physical description, rather existing in the same imageless, transcendent sense as the Upanishads' Brahman. Nonetheless, Kabir is able to direct towards transcendent Ram the same intensity of devotional feelings as does Mirabai, likening the worshipper's feelings to those of lover for beloved, baby for mother, and wife for husband. Kabir also describes in graphic terms the process by which bhakti enables seekers to burn away the dross of the self. Like Mirabai, he details the pain that burning involves, for while the path of bhakti is sustained by great love, it also requires a significant degree of consciously adopted suffering. This is because giving up the self, and seeking immersion in that which transcends the self, requires we deconstruct our self and infuse it with awareness of Brahman. It is a demanding and often painful task

For both Mirabai and Kabir, the guru plays a significant role in facilitating transformation. In her poems Mirabai acknowledges the significance of the guru as a conduit for guidance and as a source for exercises needed to practice bhakti. Kabir presents the relationship between seeker, guru and Ram in greater detail. In some forms of Indian spirituality the pupil is encouraged to view the guru as a manifestation of God, as Chaitanya's followers did with their teacher. In practical terms, this involves submitting oneself to the teacher's instructions, and carrying out whatever tasks the teacher assigns, without objection or argument. It is easy to misunderstand the intent of this practice, especially when Eastern and Western religious traditions recount stories of teachers who manifested very obvious human failings. However, the psychospiritual purpose behind this teaching of submission to the guru is to provide the student with the opportunity to bypass their limited self and learn to surrender to the higher Self.

Carrying out this task successfully presupposes that teachers have eliminated negative, ego-driven traits from their own psychology, and so have removed pettiness and personal desire from their words and actions. It also presupposes that students don't indulge in greed, vanity, self-pity, resentment, selfishness, arrogance, or any of the numerous other psychological that impede not just spiritual development, but any form of learning at all. It must have been out of frustration with the way neither teachers nor pupils measured up to this ideal attitude that Kabir wrote: "No competent gurus nor pupils I found, just players of greedy games." For, ultimately, neither the guru nor the seeker are human beings. Rather, spiritually they transcend their human form, being part of the Unmanifest that permeates the cosmos.

Ramnan is promoted by both Mirabai and Kabir. This practice involves the repetition of a name of God, or a phrase containing a name of God, whether by passing beads through the fingers, on the breath, with the heartbeat, or in the mind. Psychologically, the practice of repeating helps the seeker interupt mundane, repetitious thinking. Any name of God may be used in this exercise, because it is not the name, but the depth and intent with which it is repeated, that facilitates its effectiveness.

Prayer and mediation are advocated and practised by both poets. The inner focus that these practices require helps the seeker strengthen and purify internal energies, particularly sex energy, which the Indian tradition calls kundalini. Kundalini is transformed sex energy that feeds the seekers' energy centres. Mirabai refers to kundalini when she makes reference to the Jamuna and Ganges rivers, which symbolise the twin channels by which kundalini energy travels up the spine. It is also referred to in the final poem that begins with the phrase: "Now a high desire for God's name rises in me." The last of Kabir's poems included here, written in the genre of "upsidedown poems', is also about kundalini and its internal impact.

The reason struggle resonates throughout all Mirabai's and Kabir's poems is that it provides the means by which seekers transcend their personal self and achieve spiritual freedom. Such freedom does not liberate the seeker from the body's limitations, suffering, karma, or death. But it does raise the seeker's consciousness so that she or he may achieve a state of awareness that transcends the physical existence we experience via our body's senses.

Mirabai and Kabir not only record the intense struggle required to achieve such an experience, but in the process create intense, intelligent, emotional, and challenging poems. For us today, living in a culture flooded with materialist values and superficial religiosity, the profound spirituality at the heart of each poets' work is as relevant today as it was when they lived, loved, struggled, and overcame.

These translations

These translations were undertaken at the instigation of Shri Muniji Maharaj, while I was in Rajasthan in 1979, studying in his ashram. The translation process began with Shri Muniji selecting poems of Mirabai and Kabir from the many in circulation under each poet's name. Several thousand poems are ascribed to Mirabai, but scholars consider only around two hundred are likely to have been written by her. A similar situation applies to Kabir's work. While it is impossible today to know for certain which poems are irrefutably the work of each poet—after all, Kabir was illiterate, so others had to write down his verses, and there is no evidence that Mirabai collected her lyric poems—Shri Muniji selected those poems that, in his view, genuinely reflect each poet's artistry and spiritual perspective. He then arranged the poems to progressively take the reader deeper into each poet's outlook.

In the case of Mirabai, the most authoritative collection of her work is the *Mirambai ki Padavali*, a collection of just over two hundred poems made by Parahsuram Caturvedi. Kabir's work exists in three major collections. The oldest is the *Guru Granth*, compiled in 1603, in Punjab province. The other two collections, dating from a century later, are the *Bijak* and *Pañcvāni*, a Rajasthani collection of the poems and sayings of five saints. The following selection of Kabir's work has been made from this last collection.

Once selected and arranged into order, the poems were translated by Shri Muniji's Rajasthani pupils, under his guidance, into literal English prose translations. The literal prose translations of Mira's poems and the two Upanishads were made by B.K. Thanvi, assisted by A.R. Purohit and R.R. Sharma. Kabir's poems were translated by A.R. Purohit. These literal prose translations were then worked into the form presented here. The aim throughout has been to adhere as closely as possible to these literal translations, to retain the poems' imagery, and to reflect the original poetic forms. My aim throughout has been to reproduce the original poems' aesthetic, emotional and intellectual qualities.

The reader will note that a number of Indian words and terms have been left untranslated. In some cases this is because there is no English equivalent. But also it is useful to be reminded that what we are reading comes from a distant time, place and outlook. A glossary clarifies the meaning of these words.

Finally, I thank Sigrid Saga whose line drawings viscerally evoke the emotions and longing behind Mirabai poems and the Upanishads.

Working on these poems has been both stimulating and enjoyable. I hope they provide equally stimulating and entertaining reading.

Keith Hill

FURTHER READING

José Pereira (ed). *Hindu Theology: A Reader*. Image Books, 1976.

Mohan Singh Karki. *Kabir: Selected Couplets from The Sakhi in Transversion*. Dehli: Motilal Banarshidass Publishers, 2001.

Linda Hess and Shukdeo Singh. *The Bijak of Kabir*. Oxford University Press, 2002.

F. Max-Muller, revised by Suren Navlakha. *The Thirteen Principal Upanishads*. Wordsworth Classics, 2009.

21 Songs of Mirabai

I cannot live without you

Beloved, I cannot live without you.
I long for us to meet, yet what am I to do?

Bloomed lotus without water, night sky with no moon,
I'm a sad woman; lover, when will you return?

Anxious, anguished, I roam lost night and day.
Separation eats my heart, I cry out like one flayed.

Days I feel no hunger, nights I cannot sleep.
When I try to explain, I find my tongue won't speak.

Yet what am I to say? Talking's what strangers do.
Lover, come now and fill my being with you!

You own my soul, so why this tortuous absence?
Come to your captive and end this tearful sentence.

Mira has dedicated many lives to you.
She longs to kiss your feet—and prays you want that too!

People listen! I'm in pain

People listen! I'm in pain, the pain of a lover.
Such great pain cannot be revealed to any other.

I have a wound from which tears and sighs congeal:
only the wounded know what the wounded feel.

There's a fire in which women are burnt alive:
you must jump in yourself to know this state of mine.

What sleep is there for one whose bed's a crucifix?
Please tell me what to do, I long to find some rest.

The sky's a platform for my husband's bed, I lie down low.
Who knows where to meet him? Which way should I go?

I'm this pain's victim, I wander through forest and field:
no doctor existing has the cure by which it's healed.

Mira's pain is that of absence, God is the cause.
Her pain will be cured only when the doctor is her lord!

wander through forest and field

If you remain absent

Ramaiya! If you remain absent I shall die.

Without you all which I eat and drink is tasteless,
because of you the light is fading from my eyes.

Again and again my heart cries out its pain:
night becomes dawn, now the sun is leaving the sky.

Mira's whole being longs to meet her lord.
What a tragedy if you should choose to pass her by!

Because of you I am lonely

Husband, because of you I am destitute and lonely.
I can stand it no more, I am leaving this place.

Yet to meet my loved one, who could arrange that for me?
I would give body and soul to feel your embrace.

You're the reason that from forest to forest I flee.
Because of you I'm in disguise and hide my face.

The engagement period expired, I did not see.
Now my hair's turned grey and everything gone to waste.

Lord, when will Mira be able to say we?
She's leaving city and king—please give her just a taste!

I'm waiting, my lord

I'm waiting, my lord, and you're the one whom for.

Both eating and drinking have lost their appeal:
my sad, searching eyes have become closed doors.

Without your presence, my life gives me no pleasure;
my heart pounds constantly, agitated and sore.

Says Mira, I gave up the whole world for your sake,
so please come, my lord, and take what is yours!

How is it you're still alive?

Old weeping woman, how is it you're still alive?
Without your beloved Hari, how do you survive?

Because my husband's absent, I've become insane,
like wood attacked by worms, my body has decayed.

There's no medicine which spread will cure these sores;
nothing has effect when insanity's the cause.

The tortoise lives in the ocean, frogs in ponds and creeks,
water's their home, in water they grow and beget.

Yet take the fish out of the water and watch with your eyes:
its body flaps and flops, in a short while it dies.

I roam forest and field to hear the voice of the flute.
My husband is its source; there waits my passion's fruit.

Beloved, Mira holds herself and moans.
This separation hurts—pleasure's in your arms alone!

enter my house, o please come in

Enter my house, please come in

Absent beauty, enter my house, please come in.

I shall give to you my body, mind and property.
All these I'll offer, then sing to your grace a hymn.

You are the praiseworthy, in you all virtues reside,
but I'm without virtue, frail and black-cloaked with sin.

This cloak's ignorance, I lack the wisdom virtue brings,
whereas you are all, and generous beyond comparison.

My Hari, Mira longs to know when you and she will meet.
Her eyes are swollen; it's real pain with which they brim!

A bowed head I bring

Krishna! Salutations and a bowed head I bring.

I see you crowned with peacock feathers, forehead marked.
Hair dangles over your ears, on those ears hang rings.

Yes, and you play your flute, it's there on your lower lip.
Just to please Radha, you play melodies with silver wings.

O happy, happy Mira, that she can witness this sight.
Her brimming heart smiles. She claps her hands and sings!

Mira's tied bells to her ankles

Mira's tied bells to her ankles, see how she dances!
There's magic in her feet, and fire in her glances!

Why has such ecstasy into her been poured?
Because she declared herself the servant of the lord.

People stared and shouted she's become insane.
Those of 'high caste' said she brought her house shame.

Ranaji has sent a cup of poison for her to drink.
She drained it with a laugh and didn't even feel sick!

O Mira's beloved will never not be.
He's eternal delight, and she found him so easily!

she drained it with a laugh

Remain before my eyes

Beloved! Please always remain before my eyes.

Enter my vision and there permanently reside.
No, never leave; no forgetting nor chilling goodbyes.

I float on this world's cares without attachments or ties.
Take care of your lover so she never has cause to cry.

Ranaji has sent poison, he wants me to die.
I pray, turn this to a cup of nectar; show I don't lie.

May Mira at last meet the one she most admires.
And may there be no parting after, just love's eternal fire!

Please look at me

My Hari, please look at me—even just a glance.

I have eyes for no-one else, yet you ignore me:
why's there such a frost in the depths of your heart?

All my faith's in you, you're the only one for whom I care,
your image inflames my thoughts, none else, I swear.

Yes, I know all my aspirations towards you leap,
while you have millions, just like me, bowing at your feet.

Yet here I remain, standing, requesting with my tears.
Hurry, time passes; day became night; now dawn appears.

Immortal lord, Mira would that she becomes your bride.
Blushing, she offers all she has—her life—as bribe!

the only one for whom I care

My heart's sole destination

Lord, please do not renounce me and disappear.
You are my maharaj, my joy and only care.

I am a woman, women have the power of dust,
while you are the master and chief of all my caste.

What virtues do I have? I'm foul water in a ditch,
but you're unlimited, and can do whatever you wish.

Yes, I am yours, we are soulful relations.
To whom else can I turn but my heart's sole destination?

Mira worships Krishna, all else has her disdain.
So please come now; save her from dishonour and shame.

I shall dance

I shall dance in the presence of Krishna, my lord.
Purely to please, my bare feet will caress the floor.

So solemn and enticing, I shan't be ignored,
and as I turn, closer—to examine him—will I draw.

Yes, love's tied bells to my ankles, tinkling, so small.
And who knows? Perhaps, as I dance, all my veils will fall.

What do I care for customs and the world's joyless laws?
When he arrives, I shall silently close the door.

Yes, Mira will share her lover's bed, embraced and warm.
They'll laugh and sip love's wine—she knows she won't
        be bored!

my bare feet will caress the floor

I worship Lord Govinda

I worship Lord Govinda, from whom all virtues flow.

If a city's king displeases, they succour him,
but if my Hari displeases, what can I do?

Ranaji has sent a cup of poison to me:
convert it to nectar that my blood may not slow.

He could have sent a box, and inside a poisonous snake;
I would have seen that snake as Saligram, I know.

Mira's love is so deep it has made her mad.
She longs to have you as husband—do not leave her sad!

My lord wears a peacock crown

Move, my mind, to the banks of Jamuna and Ganges.

Towards waters so clear, into depths so holy,
let the coldness cool the fever of my body.

Krishna is there, melodiously playing a flute,
and with him is Balbeer, his smile gentle and sweet.

My lord wears a peacock crown on his head;
diamonds grace his ears, his gown's of silken thread.

What a vision! Mira's eyes will never be replete.
She declares she's in love forever and throws herself at
      his feet!

melodiously playing a flute

Ramnam is a delightful drink

Ramnam is a delightful and relishing drink.
My mind, into your inmost recesses let it sink.

Leave distracting company and sit among the good;
only they talk of and remember God, as you should.

No more of lust, pride and anger—leave these temptings;
as the stream flows on, there, not here, find enchantings.

Mira's devoted to God, he fires her ecstasy.
She's only ever soaked in bliss in his sweet company!

Do not leave this love

Friends! Do not go; do not leave this love!

Come together, join me, embracing him with your eyes,
come and discover what great joy in that vision resides!

See the beauty of Krishna, the ecstasy he gives,
come see his face, for only then can you say you've lived!

Who cares what shape or name to him you ascribe?
If one path unveils, walk it; whatever works, that try!

Says Mira, Not all seekers find what they are looking for.
Only the lucky know the joy of embracing their lord!

for only him she pines

Do not postpone your destiny

Do not postpone or avoid your destiny, my friends.

Harichand was always honest, of truth he was king,
yet water to a lower-caste man's house he had to bring.

The five Pandus had mother and Draupadi, common wife,
but the Himalayas froze their bones and all lost their life.

Bali wanted Indra's throne, so sacrificed in fire;
he was flung into the nether world—thus was he retired.

Mira worships her lord, for only him she pines,
for none but he transmutes, and makes of poison, wine.

Repeat, my mind

Repeat, my mind, the name you have learned by heart.

Say, "Ram Ramhi Ram," though you're veiled by ten
      thousand sins,
for, assuredly, ramnam will tear that veil apart.

Many lifetimes testify to the bad deeds you've done,
yet utter God's name, and watch them vanish, one by one.

Who refuses to drink nectar from a golden bowl?
Who refuses ramnam then, which so intoxicates the soul?

Says Mira, Lord God is immortal, he alone I praise.
Body and mind I give to him. Thus my debt, I repay!

I bow devotedly

I devotedly bow at my guru's feet.

Without him my life is empty and has no meaning,
for the world and all its wealth is nothing but a dream.

The worldly ocean's dried up, but that's no worry to me:
my longing's for escape, my sole desire is to leave.

Mira's hopes rest in God, there all her future lies.
Thus she seeks the guru's shelter, for only he can guide.

my sole desire is to leave

Now a high desire

Now a high desire for God's name rises in me.

Once he stole the butter of the entire world;
since then he has taken on the name 'bairagi.'

O Mohan, where you left behind the love-filled flute!
Where you abandoned the intoxicated gopi!

Your head was shaven clean, a string tied round your waist.
Mohan, they placed a cap on your head, tenderly.

But one day, enraged Yeshoda bound both your legs.
It was your stealing the butter which made her so angry!

Now, Lord Krishna, you've changed your name and shape:
as Lord Chaitanya have you continued to be.

You give the feeling of Krishna with his silken cloth,
and of Chaitanya with his string and cloth tied freely.

Mira worships this child, for in him Krishna she sees.
His name is on her tongue—may it live there constantly!

2 Upanishads

Isha Upanishad

Praise to the Self, our Lord God almighty,
complete in yourself through all eternity.
Praise to the cosmos, this star-slung body:
you too are complete in true reality.
Fully complete was your completeness born,
from that completeness did you gain your form.
But what of death? If your completeness not be?
Know completeness remains, the God-Self—he!
Om Shanti, Shanti, Shanti.
May God save us from creation's three!

What through the senses we see and we hear,
of this or that, both here and there,
it is ever filled with that almighty one.
Sacrifice your whole life to him, therefore,
a remembrance you should not ignore,
and, never attached, do what is to be done.
For all this wealth we would form in a throne,
money, children, lovers or home,
neither yours nor mine, they belong to none.
Who would hope to live for one hundred years,
but to take all the acts he bears
and worshipful place them at his lotus feet?
Because despite what others choose to say
there exists no alternative way
to escape these sufferings with which we're replete.
Bad spirits and evils of different degrees
are demons clouded, living unfree
in a darkness of troubles and unknowingness.

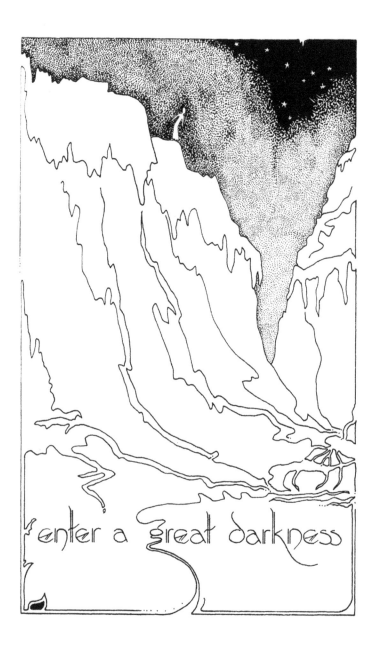
enter a great darkness

Whoever they may be who kill their self
are, after death has stolen their wealth,
repeatedly reborn into worlds of stress.

The Lord God almighty is in truth one;
immovable, who yet can run
much faster, by far, than the swiftest mind.
He is the source, the inspirer of all,
whose knowledge is bound by no wall,
who yet the senses are unable to find.
Truly, almighty God supersedes
those who run very fast indeed,
for he remains stationary, behind.
The elements' acts are like pouring rain,
creating food with which to sustain,
that humanity and all creatures survive.
The almighty God moves; he moves not;
far and further from this very spot,
yet near and ever nearer is he!
Totally mixed, like dye and water swirled,
in each molecule of the world,
yet beyond the reach of the world is he!
Who sees atman in all creatures living,
simultaneously seeing
them in God, leaves separation behind.
The seer, knowing God, feeling him in all,
living one with God and the world,
to a particular state such a one attains.
Living continuously with that state
(seeing oneness, which is that state)
he is disturbed by neither pleasure nor pain.
For, happily filled with God's enlightenment,

and free from any attachment,
he's beyond the opposites—this world's bane.

The atman is bright, with no physical
or atomic body, a crystal
brightness without artifice or attachment.
The atman knows all and is everywhere,
creator, controller of all creatures
through their karmas, since time put up its tent.
Those who worship ignorance enter
a great darkness; those proud of their
knowledge enter a far greater darkness.
But those who pursue yogic wisdom reach
ends different to those who act ignorantly—
thus the great seers who knew truth have taught us.
Who fully understands ignorance and knowledge,
worshipping knowledge and ignorance,
leaps death's hurdles and attains to deathlessness.
Those who worship the manifest world enter
a great darkness; those proud of their
worship enter a far greater darkness.
But those who worship the unmanifest reach
ends different to those who worship this—
thus the great seers who knew truth have taught us.
Who fully understands and worships both
the manifest and the unmanifest
leaps death's hurdles and attains to deathlessness.

Truth is hidden behind your leaping light.
So that it might be revealed to my sight,
I pray you, Lord Sun, please hold back your light!
Lord Sun, my God, who dark death obeys,

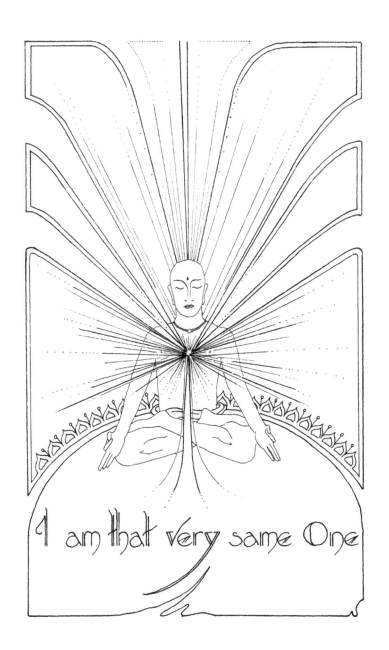

I am that very same One

I pray you kindly remove your rays,
embodied luminosity and welfare I praise.
The great truth, to whom this song is sung,
resides within you, o holy Sun.
And I myself am that very same One!
That the divine life force should inspire
the eternal elements entire,
and that this body be inflamed with fire!
My avowed mind, remember; remember
the acts done by yourself;
remember the acts done by yourself.
O Fire, knower of all acts on our part,
lift these hurdles of sin from our heart
and kindly lead us on the saving path.
Again and again we pray, again and again.
At your lotus feet bowed heads we lay;
again and ever again we pray!

Om Shanti, Shanti, Shanti!
The Lord God save us from creation's three!

Kena Upanishad

Praise to Brahman, our Lord God almighty!
All is Brahman, as the teachings state truly.
May limbs, speech, ear and eye wax mighty in me.
From my life force and senses let no strength flee.
Ever faithful to Brahman may I prove to be.
May Brahman never have cause to spurn me.
The teachings state virtues are the atman's really.
May, in atman delighting, they too reside in me.
Om Shanti, Shanti, Shanti!
The Lord God save us from Creation's three!

PUPIL
We think, yet what willed self guides and directs
the mind towards its thought objects?
Whose command causes the life force to flare?
We know mankind thinks and spouts forth in speech,
yet by whose will occurs this in each?
What intelligence aims the eye and ear?

TEACHER
Ear of the ear, there is something behind
which similarly uses mind,
eye and tongue, and the life force in all.
Discarding their self-sense to those close-curled,
and leaving behind the sensory world,
the wise, in full truth, become immortal.
Eye, mind and speech can go there not ever;
we know it perfectly never;
and we don't know how to teach about it!

For it is distinct from all that is known,
and far remote from the unknown—
thus seers who knew truth have spoken of it.
That which speech is unable to speak off,
but which through speech came to be known—
that is Brahman, not what people worship here.
That which mind found impossible to feel,
but which gave to mind its name—
that is Brahman, not what people worship here.
That which is far beyond the eyes' vision,
but because of which the eyes see—
that is Brahman, not what people worship here.
That which we can never hear through the ear,
but because of which this is being heard—
that is Brahman, not what people worship here.
That which the life force is unable to breath,
but because of which the life force is breathed—
that is Brahman, not what people worship here.
Yet who thinks he well knows, knows very little;
self-delusion makes many minds brittle.
You have yet to find what is known to you.

PUPIL
I don't think, "I know well," nor "I know not."
Yet I know too. He who knows not,
But knows what he knows not—he understands.

TEACHER
Who conceives Brahman is beyond conception,
he understands! Seers say they don't
know it, fools that they know perfectly well.
Who in and through all transformations still

to leave the sensory world

intuits it, in atman is fulfilled,
and through knowledge finds immortality.
Some find Brahman here, in this life attained.
By them the final goal is gained.
Others don't, and on them destruction falls.
Who choose to leave the sensory world behind,
and embracing atman find,
they are the wise and become immortal.
It is said Brahman once plied victory's lance
for the Devas, but in ignorance
and vainly they thought the victory theirs.
Hence Brahman, well seeing their vanity,
caused a wondrous spirit to be.
In such a form he appeared to them.
Bewildered, the Devas fiery Agni asked:
"All-knower, accept this task.
Find who that spirit is." And he agreed.
Hence straight towards that spirit he hastened.
"Who are you?" he was questioned.
"Agni, the omniscient," boasted he.
"And what power in such a nature rests"
Brahman, in that form, made request.
"To burn all that's on earth," Agni said.
So Brahman, in that wondrous spirit, cast
before this god a blade of grass
and said: "Display your power and burn this."
Agni used his strength, but without even singeing.
He returned to the Devas saying:
"I could not learn who that great spirit is."
Hence the Devas full-cheeked Vayu then asked:
"Lord of the winds, accept this task;
Who is that spirit?' And he agreed.

Thus straight towards the spirit he hastened.
"Who are you?" he was questioned.
"The treader of the skies," Vayu replied.
"And what power in such a nature rests?"
Brahman, in that form, made request.
"To blow away all that's on earth," Vayu said.
So Brahman, in that wondrous spirit, cast
Before this god a blade of grass
And said: "With your great strength blow this away."
Vayu strove hard, but there was no moving.
He returned to the Devas saying:
"I could not learn who that great spirit is."
Therefore mighty Indra the Devas then asked:
"Chief of gods, accept this task
To learn who is that spirit." And he agreed.
Thus straight towards the spirit he hastened.
But before the destination
was reached, to his surprise it disappeared!
On the same spot he saw a lovely woman—
Uma, daughter of Himavan—
and he asked her who this spirit could be.
"Brahman," she replied. "Your present greatness
achieved through victory, no less
a being than Brahman caused." Then he understood.
Thus of the gods these three have proved best,
for they approached the spirit nearest,
and they were the first to know Brahman thus.
But of all gods Indra is proved greatest,
for he approached Brahman nearest
and touched – the only one to know Brahman thus.
It approached in a flash of lightning,
and vanished in an eye's twinkling—

these are the foundation

thus is Brahman to the Devic powers.
Deep within us, in the mind's thought-breath,
it is a flash between the death
of one thought and the birth of another.
This Brahman is known as Tadvanam,
the one meditated on within.
Who knows it thus, all living creatures love.

PUPIL
Teach me, master, the knowledge that saves.

TEACHER
That knowledge we already gave:
Brahman's saving knowledge has been taught.
Austerity, restraint, and dedication
of all work—these are the foundation.
The Vedas form its limbs; truth is its abode.
Who knows this, destroying sin, finds
heavenly bliss—Brahman, which will ever be.
In truth, such a seer finds bliss indeed.

Om Shanti, Shanti, Shanti!
The Lord God save us from creation's three!

7 Poems by Kabir

On serving the guru

Sadguru is sufficient. His hand over
    my head, there is nothing I need,
for Ridhi and Sidhi are my servants,
    and mukti's close to me.

Obey the guru's words
    and all problems are resolved.
Obedience makes you immortal, fearless,
    while death loses its hold.

When attachment and misery go
    know you've met the true guru's self.
Yet rise above pain and pleasure
    and you would be the guru yourself.

The guru is compassionate,
    he's poured great kindness on me.
With his blessings, death's and rebirth's
    long chain is travelled quickly.

The guru's a true, brave warrior
    wounded from toenail to broken head.
Yet his wounds aren't seen by the eye,
    they're all inside instead.

Serving the guru is difficult,
    like walking a sword's sharp blade:
be perplexed, you fall, but stand steady
    and there's no delay.

The guru has four aspects,
    each with its own quality:
the guru is philosopher's stone and lamp,
    he's mountain and bhring.

Bowed at his lotus feet, of mukti
    the pupil begs to be taught.
The guru teaches the way is found only
    by mutually tuning thoughts.

The pupil who disobeys the guru
    —thus warns Kabir—
this pupil finds no rest, for death
    will follow him everywhere.

He who ignores the guru and his own
    stumbling course sets,
both universe and eternity desert him—
    he finds only death.

Meeting the guru, I become fearless.
    Now no desires remain
but to null myself in his words,
    confidently believing in him.

The guru's the greatest giver,
    the pupil the greatest beggar,
for the three world's estates are given
    the one by the other.

The guru's a true warrior;
    at the pupil his arrows dart.

Hold just one and fear goes, for it
    deeply pierces the heart.

Who sees the guru as mere body
    will surely go to hell:
he will be reborn a dog, birth after
    birth, sick and unwell.

Yet those who arrive and depart
    with the guru's permission,
for them, says Kabir, there will be
    no reincarnation.

Keep the guru over your head.
    Undoubting, in his words rest.
Kabir says, in the three worlds
    that pupil becomes fearless.

Dedicate your head to him
    in return for his teaching:
many fools lose themselves in proud,
    vanity-filled thinking.

"The guru is a man." Who claim this
    are ignorant and blind.
Lives difficult, ill, at the last
    they'll suffer death's bind.

Both guru and God stand before me.
    To whom should I bow first?
My thanks to the guru—through him
    I quench my God-thirst.

Bow before the guru, to him give
  millioned salutations:
just as pests don't know the bhring,
    the guru brings us to his station.

Whatever is learned at his lotus feet,
    digest it in your heart.
To love only, Kabir says, does
    the true servant hold fast.

The guru possesses all, shares are
    made according to luck.
Serve the guru truly and you'll receive
    your due portion of love.

Thus teaches the guru: beggars stand
    open-armed to death.
Don't beg of anyone.
    It's better to die than to beg.

As earth from the sky differs,
    so the priest differs from his robe:
the priest serves the guru, his robe
    denotes the frail hope of the world.

Serve the guru and all your work is
    completed, every wish bears,
nor will you drown in the whirlpools
    of karma and worldly affairs.

What will happen that day, when
    the guru lifts us by the hands?

He'll seat us beneath him, shadowed
    by his feet where he stands.

Be as one dead, though alive,
    leave the hopes of the world.
The guru will then defend us, no matter
    by what unrest we're ruled.

Kabir says, the mind has died,
    the body's feeble and drained.
How can you worship God?
    It's futile at such old age.

Guru! You're compassionate, merciful,
    and give unstintingly.
I'm trapped halfway. Lift me up.
    Sail me towards mukti!

Guru! You're the god of gods;
    give me bhakti to worship you.
I seek your mercy, that day and night
    I may serve only you.

True warriors cut off their heads,
    renounce the body's desires;
the guru's delighted when a pupil
    to this selfless state aspires.

Come and go when the guru speaks,
    as a dog obeys its master's call.
Live to the guru's dictates:
    what he gives to eat, enjoy.

It's desired the guru demand
　　nothing from the pupil.
Nonetheless, the pupil should
　　give the guru all.

Where there's guru, is no vain I,
　　where proud me, no guru—
the street of love is narrow
　　and both cannot pass through.

Kabir says the way's so thorny
　　rishis and munis sat down wearily.
That Kabir climbed so far is due
　　to the guru's mercy.

In that place where there's no rebirth,
　　neither sky nor earth,
there, says Kabir, the guru stands,
　　protecting us from hurt.

The way is walked without feet
　　—this is Kabir's message—
the city has no inhabitants,
　　the guru is without flesh.

The guru is compassionate, merciful,
　　he tends patiently.
To all creatures he comes and
　　sails them towards mukti.

Creatures are ugly, dirty, with
　　uncontrolled hearts and limbs:

only the guru redresses their lack
    and sets right their sins.

Have the guru in mind always,
    no other thoughts keep:
meditation, worship, pilgrimage—
    all converge at his lotus feet.

There's a difference between words.
    The secret's in each word.
One word cools and soothes the mind,
    another stabs a wound.

Sharp words kill. Many kings abdicated,
    unable to bear what they heard.
Only their aim is fulfilled
    who identify the true word.

The tree's very tall,
    its fruit hangs in the sky.
The few birds which taste that fruit die—
    they just seem to be alive.

Who call themselves servants, but whose
    hearts don't put their lord first,
who prefer frost to drinking water,
    how will they quench their thirst?

Kabir says, they're no true servant
    who act from selfishness,
who, wrongly-intentioned, crave
    fourfold reward for their service.

Those who, night and day,
    serve the guru mindfully,
who expect no rewards—
    for them death will never be.

I thought I was I, but now I has died
    I see I am you:
both I and you dead, two bodies only
    remain as residue.

Kabir declares: I'm now the guru's pupil,
    purified and sweet.
I'm the guru's servant's servant,
    moulded like grass by the feet.

Almighty God! I don't ask for
    Ridhi and Sidhi from you,
just bless me with daily darshan
    of the competent guru!

The entire universe is in
    the guru's possession.
We share it by luck, and luck
    arrives through serving him.

People always talk of love,
    yet it's not seen in daily life;
for true love is that in which
    you're immersed day and night.

Love's not grown in the garden,
    nor in the market sold,

but one whose head is on the earth
  quickly joins love's fold.

Don't ride two horses: either be
  a pupil serving the guru,
or selfishly clutch your pride,
  prestige, and wealth to you.

If love is in your heart, it can't
  be restrained or tied:
keep it off your tongue, it will
  surely leap from your eyes!

If you keep fearing death, you will
  never to true love attain:
be ever mindful, the home of love
  is very far away.

Whoever you are—severa, jogi, jangum,
  sannyasi or sadhu—
if you don't have love, you will
  never approach the guru.

On the grace of the guru

The guru is closer to us
    than our own family;
none gives more, no caste
    severs his servants' unity.

For atman is our caste;
    our family name is life;
the guru is our God;
    our village home, the sky.

By caste we're all guru of the universe,
    our family is God,
our dearest friend the Guru
    whose blessings never stop.

Psalms sung to the guru are endless,
    beyond pen and lips.
I'm forever in his debt
    for revealing eternity's depths.

By luck I met a competent guru or
    I'd have had only pain:
my life would have been extinguished
    like a mosquito in a flame.

Man is a mosquito: he falls into
    the flame, disintegrates.
Kabir says, the few who don't fall
    owe this to the guru's grace.

Fortunately I met a competent guru
    who gave me a new start.
He taught me morality:
    the controller's in the heart.

All creatures roam the universe
    like cows lost in the jungle:
we only ever find God through
    the guru's instruction.

I found a competent guru,
    through whom all is gained;
now both my caste and creed have been
    completely washed away.

Knowledge urged me to find a guru
    competent to teach truth:
by God's grace I was brought
    under such a one's roof.

Yet guru and God are the same,
    all else is futile fog,
and only by destroying the ego
    can we attain to God.

The guru has consoled me,
    through him was my mind inspired:
on the shores of Lake Mansarovar
    I found a sparkling diamond.

By the Guru's grace, my mind
    was stilled and consoled.

Now I know: God roams the heart.
    It's a story all living creatures follow.

This is Kabir's advice:
    sit on movement for consolation.
Practice meditation fearlessly,
    allowing no diversion.

All the universe suffers
    the ifs and buts of doubt:
only those who catch the guru's words
    ever throw doubt out.

I was sliding backwards, enmeshed
    in the world, selfish.
Midway, I met the guru:
    he gave me the lamp of knowledge.

This lamp is filled with oil,
    its wick endless and burning.
The way thus lit, I journeyed with
    the aim of not returning.

The guru has given us courage
    and a clear, pure mind.
Kabir says, many share a good crop,
    none eats in a famine.

Pleased with my efforts, the guru
    explained it thus to me:
love falls like rain which wets
    all parts of the body.

Chopad is played at the crossroads,
    my body's my opponent.
Kabir plays the game, but the guru
    teaches its rules and science.

I was in a well, sunk. The Guru's words
    lifted me out quickly.
Now when facing a well
    I can jump in fearlessly.

The guru gives both blessings and
    obligations—digest this fact.
I ignored the Kaliyug, who opposed me
    after reading my life's acts.

My millioned thanks to you, guru,
    from both heart and mind,
for you transmuted me from human
    to God in a very short time!

Say ramnam shaded by the ramnam tree.
    Kabir can't help you.
You must pacify your own mind,
    with the aid of the guru.

Dedicating your mind means the
    body must also go hence.
Kabir assures that when these are gone,
    nothing remains in the balance.

The guru's a true, brave warrior,
    from whom just one word darts:

immediately doubt dies, for it
    deeply pierces the heart.

The guru shoots many arrows inscribed
    with the word "love".
But to pierce the heart, just one
    has proved itself enough.

The guru's arrows are each anointed
    with meaningful words.
They hit my body, my dirty clothes fell:
    now naked, I'm forever cured.

The guru's weapons are: not to laugh,
    not to speak needlessly,
not to talk past the topic—these
    penetrate heart and mind deeply.

When the guru's arrow strikes
    the mouth becomes dumb,
the ears are made deaf,
    feet can no longer run.

The universe desires esteem,
    estate, profit and power.
Kabir seeks service, poverty, humility,
    and obligations to the guru.

God is in the heart, the universe's 'isms'
    are all death-marred,
so search your heart, or you too
    will end in the graveyard.

Earnestly pray your guru rub his
    words like a sharpener:
purifying heart and mind, he'll
    transform you into a mirror.

The guru is a warrior.
        He's wounded this body of mine.
Kabir says, it's only through the guru's grace
    that I am still alive.

The guru shoots his arrows at the
    correct time and place.
I'm now self-contained; troubles
    no longer leave a trace.

Kabir says, the guru teaches nothing
    but the reality of the essence.
Who knowingly grasps it becomes
    renowned throughout the universe.

During meditation an unseen presence
    gives the meditator news:
guru, before I die show me the unseen
    which is known to you!

The guru teaches us to say ramnam
    always, repeat, never cease.
Worshipping God through the guru,
    atman escapes fear and death.

In the heart exist sixty-four lamps
    and fourteen moons;

without God and guru, that abode
is to darkness doomed

On the competent guru

No competent gurus nor pupils I found,
    just players of greedy games.
All sank in maya's sea,
    for they sailed boats made of stone.

If the guru is blind, naturally
    his pupils are blind too,
and if blind lead the blind, falling
    into a well is all they can do!

I say, cut off that guru's beard whose
    teaching doesn't scythe doubt,
for not only does he sink but
    he drags his pupils down.

An incompetent guru means
    the pupil is incapable:
grasping pupil, profit-seeking guru,
    and both are in trouble.

As rain seeks no payment for filling
    reservoirs and streams,
so the guru infuses freely with
    his endless qualities.

Without a competent guru
    you'll remain an illiterate fool.
Dress like a saint, inside you're an idiot
    begging from door to door.

Without a competent guru
  you can't climb wisdom's heights.
Striding out to meet God,
  you won't manage twenty steps.

He's no true guru who can't cast
  doubt from the mind:
to find God, we need
  such a one as our guide.

The unknown lured me, I sought a guru,
  he showed me the path.
Only by obeying his teaching did I
  hit the required target.

If you've something within, play with it,
  there's no confusion—
two blind people trying to dance
  fascinates no one.

Yet what can the guru do if the pupil
  lacks that something?
Play the flute in lazy fools' ears,
  still they do nothing.

If you're stupid, it doesn't matter
  who's your guru, you'll forget:
too ignorant to use one dhoti,
  you won't be offered a full set!

On remembrance

True saints teach remembrance:
    it's the direct path.
Practised night and day, it takes you
    to the required target.

True servants remember with
    their every breath.
Non-attached, they escape
    the whirlpool of birth and death.

Suppose the body's a pouch,
    mind a rosary, eyebrows ash:
repeating within, true seers
    meet God in the worldly crush.

Ramnam is the essence of
    the entire universe.
Kabir knows that who swallows it
    radiates true eminence.

Remember with your breath and
    you increase your inner store;
with every blink of the eye
    remember, add ever more.

Ram! Give me strength to remember you
    always in heart and mind!
May I become like war-ravaged
    battlefield and jungle ruins!

Why strut the world proudly?
    Remember God and nothing else.
Why make such vibrations?
    Be one-pointed in remembrance.

The world's in love with the body,
    though daily bells chime,
for nobody likes to hear them—
    except God and mind.

Kabir says, a rosary's made of wood,
    and many styles take it round.
My preferred remembrance is with breath,
    though in it no knot's found.

I built a house in zero-space,
    pronounced each word loudly:
the light rose and made me a lamp—
    God comes out then only.

By crying, "You! You!", we become
    yourself entirely.
I have lost myself: wherever I look
    God is all I see.

"You! You!" I cried. Yourself in
    myself made permanent home.
The mind mixed with you, for there was
    nowhere else for it to go.

Five wives remember their husbands,
    the sixth remembers mind.

Knowledge lit up Kabir
    when he found Ram's diamond.

I wish only to practise ramnam,
    I wish for nothing else,
for one who forgets God
    certainly goes to hell.

I've reaped poisoned karma sown
    evilly birth after birth,
yet place sins before God and
    they vanish at a blink.

When karma's boat reaches the shore,
    sins vanish at a touch,
but repeat them and, reborn,
    the boat is swept away, lost.

Says Kabir, remember God and
    every barrier falls.
The Earth's then seen for what it is:
    sad, and very small.

Home's distant, the way difficult,
    thorns make you stumble.
So how will you reach God's presence?
    It's impossible!

The path's difficulties aren't removed
    by enumerating them.
The one way God is attained
    is by remembering him.

It's true remembrance brings difficulties,
    it brings several.
You balance on a trapeze with
    nowhere to go if you fall.

Yet, says Kabir, with love in heart and
    mind, remember constantly,
for the shore remains out of reach
    if you forget you sail God's sea.

Kabir says, it pleases God
    when the heart to him is wed.
The separate pieces reunite
    when sewn with such a thread.

All dissension comes from the mind,
    its fire burns the universe.
Extinguish mind's fire with the cool
    waters of remembrance.

Without remembrance, no knowledge,
    and fear fuels ignorance;
when curtains veil the philosophers' stone,
    no gold from iron appears.

Without fear, no emotions, and love
    requires emotion's fever.
Yet when fear runs from the heart
    all worries are gone forever.

The guru gave me mind's rosary
    through which comes knowledge:

constant remembrance without hands
is the correct practice.

Through remembrance we forget
the body's desires and cares,
but forget remembrance and
attachments bind the body again.

I never want to forget remembrance,
for life is a cord,
and death won't tighten the noose
if we remember the name of God.

Kabir says, remembrance is the essence,
nothing else has worth.
When I searched all beginnings and ends
I found only death.

Knowledge says so, the wise die saying it,
so why cling to stupidity?
Till you die, remember—
this the competent Guru taught me.

Ramnam is gold, all else is
breakable glass and tin.
Clasp this truth solely, discarding vanity
and all perishable things.

On intelligence

Intelligence has been distributed
throughout the universe;
almighty God has showered and
spread it since time began.

They're robbed of themselves who
remain ignorant of this,
but the wise face death fearlessly,
for it's in their hands.

On saints' teachings

Hear Kabir's truth: there's a difference
    between creature and universe.
Who hears this correctly
    escapes the wheel of rebirth.

Coin by coin we've saved millions
    and billions of rupees—
by the same method are nimboli
    produced on the neem tree.

Kabir has said it before: ramnam
    is the essence of the universe.
Even the gods Brahma, Vishnu and
    Shiva have confirmed this.

Only so far as you see God in
    each creature do you benefit.
If no such ray of knowledge strikes you,
    best run to a saint.

Kabir says: I have said and
    go on repeating this fact—
remember Ram, for nothing else
    can satisfy your lack.

Repeat "Ram" yourself, persuade
    others to day in and out.
The mouth that doesn't say "Ram"
    isn't worth the name mouth.

The mind keeps you dancing to
        the wishes which from it pour—
yet dance to Ram's wishes
        and you'll become immortal!

Try now to plunder ramnam to
        the greatest depths you can bear:
it's no use repenting later,
        when you're on your deathbed.

Speak sweet words always
        that not only do you glow,
but you cool others, and by
        this practice quell everyone's ego.

Remember Ram while the wick burns
        in the lamp of your body,
for when the oil expires
        you'll fall into death's sleep.

Continue to serve the guru
        that you may be blessed.
Now you're born human, serve,
        for such birth is not endless.

If you don't do so now you'll
        repent of it in old age,
but then you won't manage even
        ten steps on God's pilgrimage.

Kabir advises, remember God,
        set aside maya's poisoned seeds.

You won't necessarily be
   reborn a human being.

At old age you may plan to marry
   and call God your spouse—
but the farm is empty when the crop
   has already been reaped.

In youth you did nothing, so
   why cry now over spilt milk?
Remember God when your hair's so white?
   You're far too weak!

At adulthood lovers lured you,
   and now your back's withered, look!
Eyes and mind dull, it's pointless trying
   to read the holy books.

On separation

Waiting, watching for you so long,
    my eyes are now shadows.
Through crying, "Ram! Ram!"
    my tongue's covered with ulcers.

Tears fall from my eyes like drops
    from a well's waterwheel.
The rainbird cries for monsoon's first drops:
    awaiting Ram, that's how I feel.

The lover weeps all night like a baby
    deserted in a garden.
Kabir says, who rides love's roundabout
    emanates the light of separation.

The lover stands at the crossroads,
    asking all who walk by:
"Please give my beloved a message:
    when will he come by?"

Ram! I've longed to meet you
    for such a very long time.
My heart longs to embrace you.
    There's no rest in my mind.

Wanting darshan of Ram, the lover
    so weakened she collapsed.
Don't give me darshan after death,
    of what use is that?

Kabir says, I tell you, Ram,
    don't meet me after death.
When the iron's been destroyed,
    what use the philosopher's stone then?

The loyal woman worships her husband,
    deeply, she loves him:
thoughts of separation create knowledge
    which leads to union.

Doubts and confusions aren't stilled
    by a message or two.
They're erased only by you coming here—
    or by me nearing you.

Yet I cannot approach you.
    Nor can I invite you here.
Ram, this separation will kill me,
    heating me beyond what I can bear!

Burn this body so it turns to ash,
    the smoke to heaven rises.
Only by chance, when Ram pleases,
    do showers extinguish the fire.

Burn this body so it turns to ash,
    with this ash write "Ram".
When that's gone, use the bones as a pen,
    go on writing "Ram".

To those filled with love's pain,
    bowing at pir's tombs gives no peace:

they will only be pacified
     when darshan of God is reached.

The snake of longing dwells in the body,
     no mantra has any effect.
Such people soon die, or if they live
     others see them as insane and deaf.

The snake of longing dwells in the body,
     it wounds within:
such people don't journey anywhere,
     and eat whatever pleases them.

Longing is born of pain,
     yet it is liked—bitterly.
Then ramnam tastes very sweet,
     for death has eaten the body.

Put a wick of all creatures into
     the lamp of your body,
use your own blood as oil—
     that is how the eyes see Ram.

Don't say separation's bad,
     for it's actually a sultan,
and all hearts are a burial ground
     which lack separation.

The saints say it: God is in the heart,
     he's locked within.
Only longing supplies the key,
     and God supplies longing!

Love butchers the eyes—the meaning
    of this only the eyes understand,
for they became bloodshot
    because of their love for Ram.

When the eyes look only on God,
    from God neither divert nor dart,
when such occurs it is said
    true love consumes that heart.

Kabir says, leave laughing, make
    your heart ready for weeping.
You won't meet your dearest friend
    unless you begin weeping.

Laugh and you forget your pain,
    yet weeping saps your strength:
remembrance is like a worm that,
    inside, eats and drinks.

That worm eats the body
    —which none ever sees it do—
and when it breaks through the skin
    only a stain is left as residue.

Such worms are born of longing.
    Ao many in our presence have died.
It always ends in death,
    whatever medicines the doctors try.

None has reached God by laughing,
    they arrived only by weeping.

If God was attained by laughter,
    longing would not exist.

If God was attained by laughing,
    who would endure these pains?
But God is attained only by
    abandoning lust, desire and anger.

Not for a second will I forget you, God,
    though you're far away,
yet remembrance will only prove fruitful
    when you are here, today.

Eyes! Turn and look within
    so I may see God constantly.
When will that day come
    when darshan of God is given me?

Day passed as I waited.
    Now night has almost gone.
The lover has not found her beloved:
    her sad heart pines.

Ram! Kill me who loves you,
    or show me my self right now!
I cannot resist this pain
    even one more hour!

Why am I still alive? Why haven't I
    burnt with my beloved?
Don't misunderstand the love of a mad,
    fascinated, perplexed woman!

I'm a lover made of wood,
    I want flames to consume me,
for if left unburnt wood rots
    much too slowly.

Kabir says, mind and body dissolve
    when torched by God's fire.
The body is left unharmed,
    for flames know the target required.

Without separation, no non-attachment,
    no love without patience:
the want-filled mind is never scaled
    except through remembrance.

The eyes are active, each second
    they bring you before me.
I found neither happiness nor you
    while ruled by my self.

From mountain to mountain I roamed,
    through weeping lost my eyes,
but I found no herb growing there
    eating which I might keep me alive.

Remembering God's name
    I dissolved like salt in water:
for no other goal would we endure
    separation's torture.

True love's not graceful one moment,
    disgraceful the next;

separation visits only that heart
whose love is constant.

True love doesn't diminish then rise—
such love is tawdry.
True love doesn't quarrel one moment,
the next embrace freely.

Separation invited me
when for it I hungered.
Why sit in the tree's shadow,
fearing it won't catch fire?

In love, I died; I wasn't at the funeral
to light the bier.
The flesh rotted; I sat nearby
as the skeleton burst into fire.

Crows played with the skeleton
but found only bones,
for flesh will never be found
on the lover's skeleton.

So long I've searched, Ram.
When will you be found at last?
All my works and acts are yours;
please meet me in my heart.

Mind and body must be finally
and totally burnt.
Separation then sifts the ash for
a residue which can't be reburnt.

Burn the body, mind and youth;
    convert these into ash.
Kabir proclaims: lover, awake!
    Why still search the ash?

Don't quarrel with separation,
    my wise and gentle mind,
though it eats flesh, nerves, bones,
    and makes the body a graveyard.

Tell, how will that day be when
    Ram lifts me by my hands?
Me his personal servant, he'll seat me
    at his lotus feet where he stands.

Now you embrace my satisfied heart,
    while patience holds my mind.
But, warns Kabir, Ram cannot be met
    when sin the body defiles.

When creature's mixed with creature
    Ram cannot be spied:
neither God is met nor fire extinguished—
    I've exhausted myself trying.

Almighty God! I'm a small puddle
    and you're the endless sea.
I've waited so long: as a pond fish longs
    for the ocean, so with me.

Day and night the lover burns
    in flames he longingly endures.

Says Kabir, this fire will never cool,
for it's fanned by the competent Guru.

On the inverted world

Stay awake, seeker! Don't allow
    yourself to fall asleep!
Then death won't bite, disaster strike,
    or age sap the body.

The moon eats the sun,
    the holy Ganges sucks up the sea,
water in shadow reflects light,
    the sick kill the nine stars of destiny.

Who ever sees a tree's root?
    But those who do pluck the fruit.
Then the burrow swallows the snake
    and the earth tastes its own extract.

Seated in the cave I saw the whole universe,
    outside it I saw nothing.
The bow has shot the hunter—
    who has seen this strange happening?

Upside-down in water the pot floats,
    right way up it's sinking.
Whoever the world hates
    obtains the power to bestow blessings.

All know when rain from the sky falls
    the earth becomes wet,
but who knows when rain from the earth rises
    and the sky becomes wet?

Expert singers don't sing,
    the silent constantly sing aloud:
all see Krishna play the flute,
    but the unhearing hears the sound!

Everyone knows how to live and speak,
    the rest is an unspoken story:
the earth grabs and eats the sun—
    this is the yogi's teaching.

Look! Without a cup, evaporated water
    replenishes the river.
Kabir says only the diligent yogi
    tastes this extracted nectar.

Appendices

Glossary

Atman	Literally, self. Human beings' spiritual core.
Agni	God of fire.
Bairagi	One who has renounced the world and lives in solitude in order to engage in spiritual practices.
Balbeer	Krishna's brother.
Bali	King of the demons. The Vedas relate a story of how Bali wanted Indra's throne, but was defeated by Vishnu and banished to the underworld.
Bhakti	Devotion, worship. One of the principal paths to God.
Bhring	The black bee. It takes a larva from another species, wraps it in a cocoon, and feeds it until it is an adult when it releases it into the world. A symbol for selflessness.
Brahma	The creator God. Forms a triad with Shiva, the destroyer, and Vishnu, the sustainer.
Brahman	God, the Imperishable, the Absolute.
Chaitanya	A famous yogi who lived in the fifteenth century whose teaching emphasised love. He gave fresh impetus to the yogic tradition, which had withered. He is considered to be an incarnation of Krishna.
Chopad	An ancient dice game, played on a + shaped board.
Darshan	To be in the physical presence of another.
Devas	Vedic heavenly powers, the gods.
Dhoti	A cloth wrapped around the waist. Spiritually, it represents the act in which one gives up worldly goals and practises renunciation.
Draupadi	Common wife of the five Pandu brothers, by each

	of whom she had a son. A central character in the Mahabharata.
Ganges	The holiest river in India. When paired with the Jumuna, the two rivers refer to the raising of the kundalini (sex energy) up two channels, rising from the base of the spine to the pineal gland.
Gopi	The milkmaids in love with Krishna. On one occasion Krishna multiplied himself so each could dance with him.
Govinda	A name for Krishna, which literally means "one who has restrained the five senses".
Guru	Spiritual teacher. The four qualities Kabir gives to the guru—philosopher's stone, lamp, mountain, and bhring—respectively signify inner transformation, illumination, the heights of knowledge and selflessness.
Hari	A name for Krishna, meaning Lord.
Harichand	Indian king famed for his honesty and truthfulness. His name subsequently became proverbial.
Himavan	In Vedic mythology Himavan was the father of Uma. "Him" means ice, symbolising knowledge.
Indra	King of the devas (heavenly powers).
Jamuna	A holy river. Traditionally paired with the Ganges.
Jangum	One who has renounced home, family, possessions and occupation. The renouncer becomes a jangum, jogi, etc, depending on his or her caste.
Jogi	See jangum.
Kaliyug	The age of iron. The last of four ages according to Vedic mythology, it is the least spiritual. The present age.
Karma	Literally means work. Metaphysically, the results of any action or work. Identification with the act

of working, and attachment to the results of work done, ensure human beings are born into another body.

Mahara	Great king.
Mansarovar	Fabled lake on the border of Tibet, Nepal and India, the shores of which are said to be strewn with diamonds.
Mantra	A phrase that usually contains one of the names of God. Repetition of a mantra helps to still thought, develop concentration and focus energy.
Maya	Literally means illusion. Philosophically, the term refers to the world as experienced via the senses.
Mohan	A name for Krishna when he was young.
Mukti	Release from the rounds of births and deaths.
Munis	Yogis who have renounced the world and also undertaken a partial or complete vow of silence.
Neem	The margosa tree. Its seeds are renowned for their medicinal qualities.
Nimboli	Seeds of the neem tree.
Pandus	The five brothers whose story is told in the Mahabharata. After their victory in battle over their cousins they were forced into the Himalayas, where all perished.
Pir	A Muslim saint. A pir's tomb is highly revered due to the spiritual power considered to emanate from it, and which believers therefore visit to pay their respects, often in the expectation of receiving a reward.
Radha	Krishna's favorite among the gopis.
Ram	One of India's most popular names for God.
Ramaiya	A further name for Krishna.
Ramnam	Repetition of a mantra.

Ranaji	Mira's brother-in-law, ruler of Mewar.
Ridhi	Traditionally linked to Sidhi. Both are goddesses of fortune and wives of Ganesh, the elephant god of wisdom.
Rishis	Seers. Their pairing with munis is proverbial.
Sadhu	One who has renounced home, family, possessions and occupation. See jangum.
SadGuru	Literally, perfect teacher. Indian esoteric traditions teach that the pupil should treat the teacher as a manifestation of God and surrender to him or her in the same way that he or she is striving to surrender to God. The pupil's attitude thus becomes a disciple for breaking down the ego. The Guru then has an obligation to nurture the pupil without ego. It must be noted that the practice of submission is not the same as being psychologically dependent on the teacher.
Severa	One who has renounced home, family, possessions and occupation. The renouncer becomes a jangum, jogi, etc, depending on his or her caste.
Shiva	The destroyer God. Forms a triad with Brahma and Vishnu.
Sidhi	Traditionally linked to Ridhi.
Three worlds	The heavens, the earth, and the underworld.
Uma	Mythologically, the wife of Shiva, she symbolises knowledge of Brahman.
Vedas	The most ancient Indian religious writings.
Vishnu	The sustainer God. Forms a triad with Brahma and Shiva.
Yeshoda	Krishna's mother.
Yogi	Denotes a seeker who engages in practices that take him or her towards experiencing God.

To the reader

If you enjoyed this book, please take the time to place a review at the store from which you purchased it. This will let other readers know your thoughts on the book, and support Keith's continued work. Information about Keith's other books is available at his author website, www.keithhillauthor.com, and Attar Books, www.attarbooks.com. All books may be purchased from your favourite online store, or from your local bookstore.

This book is one of a series, *Classics of World Mysticism*. Others in the series include:

The Bhagavad Gita
A new poetic translation

An enthralling new rendering of one of the world's greatest mystic texts that achieves the rare feat of balancing spiritual insight, poetic power and philosophic accuracy.
— Peter Calvert, author of *The Kosmic Web*

On the battlefield of life, desiring to do our best, how should we act? Which values should we live by? What metaphysical outlook best explains what happens to us? How do we express our spiritual nature? And how can we stay spiritually focused in the whirl of daily life? Arjuna's searching questions, asked on the brink of a war he is loathe to fight, and Krishna's profound answers, spoken in his chariot as they survey the battlefield on which thousands will soon die, offer timeless insights into the difficulties and wonders of human existence, making the *Bhagavad Gita* one of the great works of world spirituality.

The *Bhagavad Gita* was originally written in poetry, but

is usually rendered into English. This version balances the need to present the *Bhagavad Gita's* profound concepts precisely while reproducing the original poem's dramatic and poetic power. This translation is especially successful in capturing the *Bhagavad Gita's* shifts of tone, moving from vivid descriptions of the battlefield, to the precise reasoning of Krishna's advice to Arjuna, to the sublime visionary intensity of Krishna as cosmic being. Endnotes and a glossary help readers unfamiliar with Indian culture understand the poem's mythological and philosophic references.

Psalms of Exile and Return
A journey in search of inner healing and unity

In a time that is spiritually dry for so many, this book of psalms is water in the desert. They challenge, terrify, comfort, and call us to a deep humanity.
—Allan Jones, Dean Emeritus, Grace Cathedral, San Francisco

In 587 BCE, King Zedekiah of Judah led his people in rebellion against Babylonian rule. Nebuchadnezzar responded mercilessly. His army sacked Jerusalem, destroyed the Temple, and deported thousands to Babylon. These psalms are written from the perspective of one of those exiles. They express his growing unhappiness with life as a slave, his despairing cries for help to his Lord, and his eventual escape into the wilderness. After much struggle he is reunited with his lost beloved, and together they find their way back to Jerusalem.

Inspired by the passionate writings of the ancient Jewish prophets and poets, and in harmony with the Jewish healing tradition of *tikkun olam*, these poems recount the spiritual journey seekers make as they strive to transcend everyday life, enter their own hurt heart, heal its pain, and experience the wisdom that exists there. It is the story of exiles who, lost and despairing, rediscover themselves in joy.

Interpretations of Desire
Mystical love poems by the Sufi master, Ibn 'Arabi

Keith Hill's artful and beautiful renditions will bring Ibn 'Arabi's neglected masterpiece to a new readership.
—Nile Green, author of *Sufism: A Global History*

In 1201, Shaykh Muhyiddin Ibn 'Arabi arrived in Mecca. Among the many people who impressed him one drew his attention above all others: Nizám, the daughter of a prominent religious teacher. As Beatrice did for Dante, Nizám soon inspired a sequence of love poems that are Ibn 'Arabi's poetic masterpiece, *Tarjumán al-Aswáq* (*The Interpreter of Desire*).

Muhyiddin Ibn 'Arabi was known as Shaykh al-Akbar (the Greatest Shaykh), a title given him due to his profound knowledge as a mystic, theologian, philosopher and legalist. Scholars are devoting much labour to translating and interpreting Ibn 'Arabi's voluminous prose writings, but his poetry remains little known by Western readers compared with that of his fellow Sufis, Rumi, Attar and Hafiz.

This collection reveals that with his intense feeling, vivid imagery, and the playful way he reworked the conventions of Bedouin desert poetry, Ibn 'Arabi wrote poems that deserve to be placed alongside the best of his illustrious Sufi compatriots. Keith Hill's engaging new English language versions will be welcomed not just by those attracted to Sufi literature, but by all who enjoy enchanting love poetry.

CPSIA information can be obtained
at www.ICGtesting.com
Printed in the USA
LVHW051119030322
712397LV00011B/1019